WHY TRUMP SHOULD TRIUMPH
The Next Four Years of Power

By Michael Cage

LICENSE PAGE

Library of Congress © Cataloging-in Publication Data Howard West Books 2024. Why Trump Should Triumph/ Howard West Books p. cm. References contained within each chapter. ISBN 9798343917598 Copyright 2024 by Illuminated Publishing. All rights reserved.

Contents

"There's nothing more important than our republic, and our republic hinges on honest, fair elections. That's why we must vote."

"Your vote is your voice, and it's the most powerful tool you have to shape the future of our great nation. Don't let anyone take that away from you."

"The only way we lose is if we let them take away our right to vote. That's why it's critical that every patriot goes to the polls."

Donald J. Trump

CHAPTER 1: A PROVEN TRACK RECORD

In a world of promises, a proven track record is the only currency that matters.

A reputation is supposed to grow better with every step of your proven track record. But this is not the case for our former President Donald Trump. It seems during his four years as President, the more improvements he made for the country, the more he was ridiculed and ostracized to the point it seemed he could do no good in some people's eyes. Why is that?

The Media

The first thing the reader should understand is, in reference to what goes on in the world; the news media creates the narrative for what most people believe in. Below is a list of the top seven most viewed new media outlets in America. As you examine the list you will find only one of the seven is a Republican outlet. Six out of seven of them are Democratic outlets.

- **CNN** – Often viewed as leaning liberal or Democratic, with coverage that tends to align more with progressive or centrist Democratic viewpoints.
- **The New York Times** – Known for investigative journalism and reporting that often aligns with liberal or Democratic values.
- **The Washington Post** – Tends to lean liberal or Democratic, particularly on social and political issues.
- **Fox News** – Widely seen as conservative and aligned with Republican viewpoints, particularly among its commentators and primetime programming.
- **ABC News** – Often viewed as centrist but leaning slightly toward liberal or Democratic perspectives in its coverage, especially in comparison to more conservative outlets.
- **CBS News** – Similarly seen as centrist but with a slight liberal/Democratic tilt, particularly in its reporting on social and political issues.
- **NBC News** – Considered centrist to slightly liberal, with coverage that tends to align with mainstream Democratic views on certain issues.

THE MEDIA'S INFLUENCE

The powers that be have for a long time mastered the art of shaping public opinion through media to serve their agenda, a practice dating back over one hundred years. For over a century, American news media has influenced and guided the minds of the Americans.

In these modern times of ours, there's a particularly powerful group whose name I dare not mention for fear of my book being shutdown (band), blocking it from reaching you. This group, or power that be, is fairly a new power in America (some 150 years in the making).

And their influence extends to an array of powerful tools—controlling the newspaper industry, dominating radio and music, owning Hollywood, and steering the flow of information through major news media outlets. These instruments serve not just to inform, but to captivate and, at times, enchant the masses, molding collective consciousness to their design.

They have obligated themselves with the task of preparing the political, philosophical, and cultural groundwork for the establishment of what is called in some circles, a New World Order.

A GREAT DISCONNECT

In 2024, a significant disconnect exists between reality and public perception. Over the past century, especially with the rise of social media, the influence of the media has profoundly distorted societal thinking.

As early as 1922, bestselling author and commentator Walter Lippmann boldly exposed the deceptive practices of this power, revealing how they have long used media to shape and manipulate public opinion in America. In his bestselling book "Public Opinion" he wrote:

"For the most part we do not first see, and then define, we define first and then see"
Public Opinion, Quote from Author Walter Lippmann

Lippmann suggested that our perceptions are shaped by preconceived notions, and we often interpret the world based on these prior definitions rather than objective reality. This underscores the importance of differentiating between factual truth and the way news is presented, reflecting the power of media in shaping public opinion.

Lippmann understood that the images and ideas people hold are often not accurate reflections of the real world, but rather constructs influenced by external forces.

They who hold and control Hollywood, the music industry and almost all major news and social outlets – like so many nickels and dimes in their pockets; has understood for a long time that opinion for most people is formed through a complex, unconscious process rather than through deliberate, rational analysis.

Cultural influences shape our perceptions and create stereotypes that influence how we interpret the world and act in it. People act not on direct knowledge but on the mental images and ideas they have received. Public opinion is more easily swayed by emotions and symbols than by logical discourse.

Trump's Achievements (2017-2021)

During his presidency, Donald Trump achieved a number of significant policies and initiatives that's worthy of highlighting. Here are 10 of the key accomplishments attributed to Trump and his administration, 10 achievements the Left news media outlets showed minuscule coverage of:

1. Tax Cuts and Jobs Act (2017):
The Trump administration passed a significant tax reform law that lowered corporate tax rates from 35% to 21%, aimed at stimulating economic growth, job creation, and higher wages. It also included tax cuts for individuals, though these were temporary.

2. Criminal Justice Reform (First Step Act, 2018):
Trump signed the **First Step Act**, a bipartisan criminal justice reform law that sought to reduce mandatory minimum sentences for certain non-violent offenses and improve rehabilitation programs for inmates.

3. Record Low Unemployment:
Before the COVID-19 pandemic, the U.S. experienced record-low unemployment rates under Trump, particularly for African Americans, Hispanics, and women. Job growth remained strong in many sectors.

4. Economic Growth:
Trump's economic policies, including deregulation and tax cuts, led to significant GDP growth before the pandemic, with some of the highest economic indicators in decades. The stock market also reached record highs during his tenure.

5. Judicial Appointments:
Trump appointed three conservative justices to the U.S. Supreme Court (Neil Gorsuch, Brett Kavanaugh, and Amy Coney Barrett), shifting the court's ideological balance. He also appointed hundreds of federal judges to lower courts, impacting the judiciary for years to come.

6. Deregulation:
Trump pursued a robust agenda of rolling back federal regulations, particularly in industries such as energy, healthcare, and finance, with the aim of fostering business growth and reducing governmental burdens.

7. Middle East Peace Deals (Abraham Accords, 2020):
His administration brokered historic peace agreements between Israel and several Arab nations, including the UAE, Bahrain, Sudan, and Morocco, known collectively as the **Abraham Accords**, aimed at normalizing relations and promoting peace in the Middle East.

8. Rebuilding the U.S. Military:
Trump prioritized military spending, leading to increased defense budgets and the modernization of the U.S. armed forces. His administration emphasized rebuilding military readiness, increasing troop numbers, and investing in advanced technologies.

9. Energy Independence:
Under Trump, the U.S. became the world's largest producer of oil and natural gas, achieving energy independence. His administration rolled back environmental regulations and promoted domestic drilling and energy exploration, including in federal lands and offshore.

10. Trade Agreements:
Trump renegotiated several trade agreements, including replacing NAFTA with the **USMCA** (United States-Mexico-Canada Agreement), which aimed at more favorable terms for U.S. businesses and workers. His administration also pursued a tough stance on trade with China, imposing tariffs to address issues like intellectual property theft and trade imbalances.

If this book was long enough, I could sight many other things accomplished by our former president. These achievements, while notable, were met with criticism by his political advisories and the media platforms they operate through.

CHAPTER 2: HE DOESN'T PLAY THEIR GAME

Why do the Hillary, Obama, Biden and (now) Harris administrations despise Donald Trump? Is it not because he doesn't share their political objectives and ideologies for the future of this country of ours. Where Trump wants to bring back integrity to America (i.e. people living by a set of traditional values and principles,) the Harris/Biden administration is ripping the integrity from the fabric of the nation by pushing for illegal immigrant's rights and setting up a multi-sex genderizing culture.

The integrity of America is at Stake

In the heart of America's great experiment, integrity is not just a word—it's the very foundation of the nation's soul. It's the glue that holds the country's values, principles, and traditions in place, guiding each generation to navigate the complexities of freedom and democracy. Where Donald Trump seeks to revive and reinforce that integrity—rooted in long-standing beliefs of personal responsibility, and moral clarity—the Harris/Biden administration is tearing it apart, brick by brick, with policies that cater to fringe ideologies and disregard the basic tenets that have kept this country strong.

The word "integrity" itself calls to mind a consistency of values; a life lived by a set of guiding principles that are uncompromising. For America, these principles have long included the sanctity of borders, and a clear understanding of identity—both as individuals and as a nation. Yet, under the Biden-Harris administration, there has been an unprecedented shift. The steady release of millions of illegal immigrants, coupled with the aggressive push to normalize gender fluidity at the cost of traditional values, has put the country's moral and societal fabric at risk of tearing.

The Erosion of Borders and Erosion of Integrity

To understand the full impact of the Harris/Biden policies on immigration, one must look no further than the staggering numbers: According to U.S. Customs and Border Protection, in 2021 alone, over **1.7 million** encounters were reported at the southern border, a record-breaking number of illegal crossings. By the end of 2022, this number surged to nearly **2.4 million**. Where previous administrations sought to uphold the integrity of the nation's borders, the Biden-Harris approach has undermined the very notion of lawful immigration.

CONSEQUENCES

The consequences of this mass influx are clear. Communities in border states like Texas and Arizona have faced increasing pressure on their resources, from healthcare systems to public safety. A report by the **Federation for American Immigration Reform (FAIR)** estimated that illegal immigration cost U.S. taxpayers approximately **$151 billion annually**, an astronomical rise from previous years. But the cost isn't just financial. The flood of illegal immigrants has brought with it increased crime rates in some areas. In Texas alone, state law enforcement arrested over **239,000 illegal immigrants** from 2011 to 2021, many of whom were involved in drug trafficking and violent crimes.

But more than statistics, it is the principle of integrity that has been damaged. If a nation cannot maintain its borders, can it truly maintain its identity? Trump understood this, and his policies aimed at strengthening border control and enforcing immigration laws were seen as necessary steps in preserving America's sovereignty. Under his administration, illegal border crossings had reached **historic lows**. By contrast, the Biden-Harris administration has embraced policies that encourage open borders, rewarding lawlessness with amnesty and undermining the legal immigrants who waited their turn and followed the rules.

Gender Confusion and a War on Tradition

Just as concerning, however, is the administration's aggressive promotion of gender ideology, particularly as it relates to children. Across the country, school districts have been pressured to adopt "inclusive" policies that, in the name of progress, seem to strip away the clarity of traditional gender roles. This is not just a theoretical debate—real policies are being implemented that have a profound effect on the lives of children and families.

GENDER NEUTRAL BATHROOMS

In states like California and Illinois, for instance, gender-neutral bathrooms have been mandated in public schools, sparking outrage from parents and communities. The **California Healthy Youth Act**, signed into law in 2016 and further expanded in recent years, requires schools to teach students about gender identity and sexual orientation as early as kindergarten. This push has been met with resistance from parents who feel their rights are being eroded in favor of a radical agenda. In a 2022 **Gallup poll**, over **60% of Americans** expressed concerns about the promotion of gender ideology in schools, with many fearing that children are being indoctrinated rather than educated.

The reality is that many Americans are not opposed to individual freedom of expression, but they take issue with the idea that traditional gender norms—those that have been foundational in human societies for millennia—are now being vilified as outdated or harmful. Trump's America was one where personal choice was respected, but it was always understood that some values—such as the distinction between male and female—were non-negotiable. The Harris/Biden administration, however, has championed policies that blur those lines, creating confusion where there was once clarity.

A Nation in Chaos

Without integrity, a nation cannot stand. The policies of the Harris/Biden administration, from immigration to gender identity, reflect a rejection of the very values that built America. The American people have noticed. In a 2023 poll by **Pew Research**, nearly **70% of Americans** expressed dissatisfaction with the direction of the country, citing concerns over both immigration and the changing cultural landscape.

CROSSROADS

There is a growing sense that America is at a crossroads. Will the nation embrace a return to the principles of integrity, responsibility, and clear-defined thinking that Trump championed? Or will it continue down a path of division and chaos, where rules are bent, traditions are discarded, and the truth is whatever one wants it to be?

TRUMP'S COMMITMENT

Trump's legacy, and the reason why so many believe he should triumph once again, is his unwavering commitment to the idea that some things are worth preserving. A nation's borders, its traditions, and its moral compass must remain intact if it is to survive and thrive. He understood that integrity is not a relic of the past, but the key to a stable and prosperous future.

Under Trump, America was on a path to restoring its greatness. Under Harris and Biden, that greatness is being unraveled.

CHAPTER 3: A HEART OF PATRIOTISM

The presidency of Donald J. Trump has been nothing short of a battle, fought on multiple fronts, against forces that seem determined to break him. It has been a fight not for power, but for the heart of a nation he loves dearly. A billionaire by all definitions of success, Trump could easily be living a life of luxury—enjoying his wealth, his family, his accomplishments—yet here he is, in the trenches, waging war to protect the integrity of a country spiraling toward chaos under the Harris-Biden administration. This is not the story of a man chasing legacy or fame. It's the story of a man whose devotion to America is so profound that he has endured more trials than any leader in modern history. It takes a heart of patriotism to withstand what Donald Trump has faced.

The Trials of Donald Trump

Since his entry into politics, Donald Trump has been under constant fire. The minute he descended the golden escalator in Trump Tower in 2015 to announce his candidacy, the elite political class, media, and opposing forces set their sights on him. They ridiculed him, labeled him a political outsider unfit for office, and made it clear that he was not welcome in their world. But that was just the beginning.

THE RUSSIA SCANDLE

As president, Trump's bold, unorthodox approach upset the status quo. From day one, he was targeted by a media complex determined to undermine him at every turn. The Russia investigation, which consumed the early years of his presidency, was a well-orchestrated effort to delegitimize his administration. After years of endless headlines and accusations, the investigation turned up no evidence of collusion. But the damage had already been done. The media ran with it, stoking division and casting a dark shadow over his presidency.

IMPEACHED TWICE

And it did not stop there. Trump faced two impeachments—the first president in history to be impeached twice. The first was based on a phone call with Ukraine, the second on the events of January 6th. Both efforts were as much about discrediting him as they were about wounding his supporters. Trump emerged from both impeachments acquitted, but not unscathed. Each trial, each accusation, each headline cost him something, whether it was his reputation, his financial standing, or a sliver of his soul.

FELONY CASES

The felony cases, too, are something no other president has had to face. Trump has been dragged into courtrooms, labeled a criminal, and accused of everything from tax fraud to mishandling classified information. These are not small slights. These are serious charges that threaten his freedom and his legacy. Yet, through it all, he has stood firm, proclaiming his innocence, confident that the truth will prevail. The legal fees, the endless court battles, the attacks on his family— all of this could crush a lesser man. But Trump's heart beats for America, and so he fights on.

THE RACISM LABEL

Perhaps one of the most damaging accusations leveled against Donald Trump is the charge of racism. It is a label that carries weight, one that can permanently tarnish a person's legacy. Trump has been called a racist in both the media and by political opponents, despite his track record of policies that benefited all Americans, including minorities. Under his administration, unemployment rates for African Americans, Hispanics, and other minority groups hit record lows. The **First Step Act**, a groundbreaking piece of criminal justice reform legislation, helped address longstanding racial disparities in sentencing.

Yet, the label sticks. To this day, Trump is portrayed by some as a symbol of division. But those who know his heart understand that he fought to uplift every American, regardless of race or background. The accusations of racism are not rooted in truth but in a strategic effort to tarnish his image. And despite knowing that the label is false, Trump continues to endure it, knowing that history will eventually tell the full story.

A Billionaire's Sacrifice

What makes Trump's journey even more remarkable is what he has sacrificed along the way. Unlike career politicians who have little to lose, Trump has sacrificed a fortune, his business empire, and a peaceful retirement. The New York Times reported that he lost **$700 million to $1 billion** during his presidency, as his business suffered from both the legal and public relations battles he fought. His brand, once synonymous with luxury and success, has taken a hit due to his foray into politics.

Yet, he presses on. Here is a man who could be on a yacht in the Mediterranean or enjoying his golden years in Mar-a-Lago, surrounded by his children and grandchildren. He could have easily walked away from the chaos of Washington, but he didn't. He wouldn't. Because for Donald Trump, the fight for America is worth more than all the money in the world. His fortune pales in comparison to the principles he stands for.

THE ASSANSSINATION ATTEMPT

In 2020, during his re-election campaign, Trump faced a real and terrifying assassination attempt. A package containing ricin, a deadly poison, was intercepted by law enforcement before it reached him. It was a stark reminder that his life is constantly in danger, and that some are willing to go to extreme lengths to silence him. And still, he continues. This is not the behavior of a man who is in it for power or prestige. This is the behavior of a man who loves his country so deeply that he's willing to put his life on the line for it.

THE WEAPONIZATION OF GOVERNMENT

What makes Trump's continued perseverance even more astounding is the fact that he is not just facing political opponents, he is facing the full weight of a weaponized government. The Harris-Biden administration, with its ties to the deep state, has used every tool at its disposal to try to destroy Trump. From launching investigations to leaking damaging information to the media, they have sought to discredit him in ways that are unprecedented in American politics.

These are tactics more suited to a dictatorship than a democracy. Yet Trump has faced them head-on, refusing to back down. The relentless pursuit of Trump by government institutions has not only damaged his reputation but has also eroded trust in these institutions among many Americans. The FBI, the DOJ, and other once-respected agencies have been seen as tools used to bring down a political opponent. This, too, is a part of

Trump's fight—to restore integrity to the institutions that are supposed to serve the American people, not destroy them.

A Heart of Courage and Patriotism

So why does Donald Trump keep fighting? Why doesn't he retire, as many of us might wish for him? After all, he is in his late 70s, a man who has fought war after war, trial after trial, for years. He has endured slander, legal battles, assassination attempts, and countless personal attacks. He could walk away, and no one would blame him.

I, too, feel his pain. I pity him in many ways. A man who has given so much of himself, who has endured so much suffering, deserves peace. He deserves the chance to spend his remaining years enjoying life, without the government trying to destroy him at every turn. He has already done more for America than most could ever dream of, and part of me wishes he would simply let it go—retire from politics and spend his days in the company of his beloved family.

But I know he won't. He won't because he loves this country too much to walk away. He won't because he knows that the fight is far from over. As bad as things are under the Harris-Biden administration, Trump believes that America can still be saved. He knows it won't be easy, and that the damage done in four years cannot be undone overnight. But his heart beats for this nation. His patriotism is unmatched, and it is that love that drives him forward.

Donald Trump is not just fighting for himself. He is fighting for every American who believes in this country's greatness, who believes in its founding principles, and who knows that without integrity, law, and order, America cannot stand.

It takes courage. It takes resilience. But most of all, it takes a heart of patriotism, and in Donald Trump, we see that heart in full.

CHAPTER 4: THE ECONOMY, THEN AND NOW

There was a time in recent memory when America stood tall, with an economy that was booming, jobs returning to our shores, and optimism spreading across the nation. This was the America under Donald J. Trump, a leader who put the country first, focusing on economic growth, job creation, and restoring pride in what it meant to be American. Then, in 2020, came a pivotal election, and the course of America shifted dramatically under Joe Biden and Kamala Harris. What we have witnessed since is a stark contrast between an administration that prioritized the well-being of Americans and one that seems to have lost its way.

Under Trump, America thrived economically, but under Biden and Harris, the country finds itself stumbling. This is not just political rhetoric—it's a fact supported by countless examples. As we delve into the comparisons between the economy then and now, it becomes clear: Donald Trump built something great, and the current administration is slowly tearing it down.

Trump's Economic Legacy: A Foundation of Strength

During Donald Trump's presidency, the American economy experienced some of the most impressive growth seen in decades. Before the pandemic hit, the economy was setting record after record. Unemployment reached a 50-year low, with minority groups—African Americans, Hispanics, and Asians—benefiting from unprecedented job creation. The stock market reached historic highs, giving Americans with 401(k) plans and retirement accounts newfound hope for the future. Under Trump, businesses flourished, and he encouraged companies to bring back manufacturing jobs that had been outsourced for years. He wasn't afraid to get tough on trade deals, either, renegotiating agreements like NAFTA and replacing it with the **United States-Mexico-Canada Agreement (USMCA)**, which put American workers first.

One of Trump's key accomplishments was his massive tax overhaul, which slashed corporate tax rates and gave businesses the freedom to reinvest in the economy. This wasn't just a gift to the wealthy, as critics claimed. It led to real wage growth, particularly for low and middle-income workers. In fact, wages were rising fastest for blue-collar workers, bringing tangible benefits to everyday Americans who had felt left behind for years.

BIDEN/HARRIS; ECONOMIC DECLINE

Fast forward to the Biden-Harris administration, and what was once a strong, thriving economy has become a shell of its former self. Inflation has skyrocketed under Biden's leadership, driving up the cost of living for everyone, especially the middle class and working poor. Gas prices, food prices, housing costs, everything is more expensive, squeezing families who were once thriving under Trump's policies. The administration's reckless spending has ballooned the national debt, with the **American Rescue Plan** and the **Inflation Reduction Act** being prime examples of how they've prioritized government control over economic freedom. Instead of stimulating growth, these measures have fueled inflation and stifled innovation. Businesses are feeling the burden, and, as a result, job creation has slowed, and investments have dried up.

Kamala Harris, in her role as vice president, has done little to stem the tide of economic decline. In fact, her contribution to the economy has been largely absent. Her slogan, "Turning the Page," was meant to signal a new chapter for America, but in reality, it's been nothing more than empty rhetoric. Over three years into her tenure as vice president, things haven't gotten better—if anything, they've gotten worse.

Harris claims to support the working class, but where are the results? Instead of building on the economic momentum Trump left behind, she has supported policies that have done the opposite, from pushing for higher taxes on businesses to endorsing regulations that strangle innovation. Harris speaks about turning the page, but instead of progress, it feels as though the Biden-Harris administration has been flipping backward through the pages of economic failure.

Kamala Harris: A Career of Empty Promises

It's worth noting that both Joe Biden and Kamala Harris have been entrenched in the political world for decades, and yet, neither has left behind a legacy of significant accomplishment. Biden has been in Washington for over 40 years, and Harris, as a senator and now vice president, has done little to move the needle in a positive direction for the states she has represented or the nation. In fact, both have left a bad taste in the mouths of those they were supposed to serve.

Kamala Harris, in particular, has a troubling track record of changing her positions on key issues. During her 2020 presidential campaign, Harris supported **Medicare for All**—a radical policy that would have eliminated private health insurance for millions of Americans. But when she was chosen as Biden's running mate, her stance shifted. Suddenly, she was more cautious, careful not to alienate voters who supported private insurance. This is just one example of her political opportunism. In fact, Harris has shifted her stance on everything from criminal justice reform to immigration, tailoring her positions to fit the political climate rather than standing firm on any particular principle.

Contrast that with Donald Trump, who has been remarkably consistent in his policy positions. For decades, Trump has advocated for the same basic principles: putting America first, strengthening the economy, reducing government overreach, and prioritizing the American worker. His consistency, even when it was unpopular, speaks to his integrity. He doesn't change his beliefs to fit the political moment—he leads based on what he believes is right for the country.

HARRIS' EMPTY FIRST-TIME HOMEBUYER PROGRAM

One of Kamala Harris' latest promises is to provide first-time homebuyers with a $25,000 grant toward their home purchase. On the surface, this sounds like a great idea—a way to help Americans achieve the dream of homeownership. But when you dig deeper, the promise quickly falls apart. Harris plans to fund this program by increasing taxes on wealthy corporations. Yet, many of these same corporations are the ones endorsing her and the Biden administration. If her plan were truly to leave these corporations with less money, why would they continue to support her?

The truth is that Harris' proposal is nothing more than another empty promise designed to win over voters without any real intention of following through. If there's one thing the American people have learned from this administration, it's that talk is cheap, and promises are rarely kept. Under Trump, however, promises made were promises kept. He promised to cut taxes, and he did. He promised to bring back jobs, and he did. He promised to strengthen the military, and he did. With Trump, the American people got results. With Harris and Biden, they get hollow rhetoric.

The Real Impact on America

The economic decline under Biden and Harris isn't just about numbers on a spreadsheet—it's about real lives. Families are struggling to make ends meet, small businesses are closing their doors, and the American dream feels further away than ever before. Parents worry about affording groceries and gas, while retirees fear their savings won't last. Under Trump, Americans had hope. Under Biden and Harris, they have anxiety.

In key swing states like Pennsylvania, Ohio, and Michigan, voters who once supported Democrats are now questioning whether Biden and Harris truly have their best interests at heart. These states, which were pivotal in Trump's 2016 victory, have been hit hard by the economic downturn. Manufacturing jobs, which Trump worked tirelessly to bring back, are once again under threat as businesses face higher taxes and stricter regulations.

The contrast between the two administrations couldn't be clearer. Under Trump, America was strong, confident, and prosperous. Under Biden and Harris, the country is floundering, burdened by inflation, a shrinking labor market, and a loss of faith in the government's ability to lead.

A CHOICE FOR AMERICA

As we look ahead to the future, the choice is clear. Do we want to continue down the path of economic decline, or do we want to return to the days when America was winning again? Trump has proven that he knows how to lead an economic resurgence. His track record speaks for itself, and his policies put America on a path to prosperity. Biden and Harris, on the other hand, have only led us further into uncertainty and struggle.

It's time to turn the page, but not in the way Kamala Harris envisions. It's time to turn the page back to a time when America was strong, prosperous, and full of hope. That is what Donald Trump offers—a return to greatness, a chance for every American to thrive once again.

With Trump, we don't get empty promises—we get results. And for America, that's exactly what we need.

CHAPTER 5: A VIEW INTO POLICIES

Here's a breakdown of the top ten policies Republicans and Democrats typically stand for, based on general political platforms of the two major parties in the U.S.:

Top 10 Republican Policies

1. **Lower Taxes**

Republicans prioritize lowering taxes to spur economic growth, arguing that lower taxes increase individual and corporate savings, which in turn stimulates investment and job creation. They often support tax cuts for both individuals and businesses.

2. **Limited Government**

Republicans advocate for a limited federal government, where the government's role in individuals' lives and the economy is minimized. This means reducing regulations, cutting government spending, and decentralizing power to state and local governments.

3. Second Amendment Rights

Republicans strongly defend the right to bear arms, believing in the protection of the Second Amendment. They oppose many forms of gun control and advocate for individual gun ownership rights.

4. Free Market Capitalism

Republicans believe in free-market principles and oppose excessive government intervention in the economy. They support deregulation to allow businesses to operate with fewer restrictions, which they believe promotes innovation and growth.

5. National Security

Republicans prioritize a strong national defense and often support increased military spending. They believe in securing borders, combating terrorism aggressively, and maintaining a strong presence globally to protect U.S. interests.

6. Immigration Reform

Republicans generally advocate for stricter immigration policies, emphasizing the enforcement of current laws, building stronger borders, and opposing policies that they believe encourage illegal immigration, such as sanctuary cities or pathways to citizenship for undocumented immigrants.

7. **Traditional Family Values**

Republicans often support policies that promote traditional family structures. This includes opposition to same-sex marriage, opposition to abortion, and support for religious liberties as they relate to family and community life.

8. **Energy Independence**

Republicans focus on achieving energy independence through the expansion of domestic energy production, particularly in fossil fuels like oil, natural gas, and coal. They often advocate for rolling back environmental regulations that limit energy exploration.

9. **Health Care Deregulation**

Republicans oppose government-run health care systems, preferring private-sector solutions. They seek to repeal or modify the Affordable Care Act (Obamacare), arguing that it increases costs and decreases the quality of care.

10.**Judicial Originalism**

Republicans often favor judges and justices who interpret the U.S. Constitution as it was originally written, opposing the idea of a "living constitution" that evolves with societal changes. They tend to support conservative judicial appointments.

Top 10 Democrat Policies

1. **Progressive Taxation**

Democrats support a progressive tax system, where the wealthy pay a higher percentage of their income in taxes. They advocate for higher taxes on the rich and corporations to fund public services like education, health care, and social programs.

2. **Health Care for All**

Many Democrats advocate for universal health care, either through expanding the Affordable Care Act or implementing a single-payer system, such as Medicare for All. They believe health care is a right and should be accessible to everyone, regardless of income.

3. **Climate Change and Environmental Protection**

Democrats prioritize addressing climate change and promoting environmental protection. This includes supporting policies like the Green New Deal, investing in renewable energy, and enforcing stricter environmental regulations on industries to reduce carbon emissions.

4. **Gun Control**

Democrats generally support stronger gun control measures, such as universal background checks, banning assault weapons, and implementing red-flag laws to prevent gun violence. They believe stricter regulations are necessary to reduce gun-related incidents.

5. LGBTQ+ Rights

Democrats are strong advocates for LGBTQ+ rights, including same-sex marriage and anti-discrimination protections in employment, housing, and public services. They also support the right of transgender individuals to access gender-affirming medical care and bathrooms aligned with their gender identity.

6. Social Justice and Equality

Democrats focus on policies that promote racial, gender, and economic equality. This includes supporting affirmative action, criminal justice reform, and measures to reduce income inequality. They often push for reforming the policing system to address racial disparities.

7. Pro-Choice (Abortion Rights)

Democrats are firmly pro-choice, supporting a woman's right to access abortion services. They advocate for protecting the **Roe v. Wade** decision and oppose any attempts to limit or ban abortions.

8. Immigration Reform

Democrats typically support comprehensive immigration reform, including pathways to citizenship for undocumented immigrants, protection of DACA recipients (Dreamers), and opposing harsh enforcement measures like family separations at the border.

9. Workers' Rights and Unions

Democrats support strengthening workers' rights and protecting labor unions. They advocate for higher minimum wages, expanding worker protections, and making it easier for employees to join unions and bargain collectively.

10. Expanding Access to Education

Democrats push for more accessible and affordable education, including proposals like tuition-free public college and increased funding for K-12 schools. They believe investing in education is essential for economic mobility and addressing inequality.

Key Contrasts Between the Two Parties:

- **Economy & Taxes**: Republicans focus on reducing taxes and deregulation, while Democrats advocate for higher taxes on the wealthy to fund social programs.
- **Health Care**: Republicans prefer market-based solutions, while Democrats push for expanded government involvement or universal health care.
- **Gun Control**: Republicans defend the Second Amendment rights, while Democrats favor stricter gun control measures.

- **Immigration**: Republicans seek stronger border enforcement, while Democrats support pathways to citizenship for undocumented immigrants.
- **Social Issues**: Republicans lean towards traditional family values, while Democrats advocate for LGBTQ+ rights, gender equality, and reproductive rights.

Make America Great Again Bulletin

President Trump's 20 CORE PROMISES
TO MAKE AMERICA GREAT AGAIN!

1. Seal the border and stop the migrant invasion
2. Carry out the largest deportation operation in american history
3. End inflation, and make america affordable again
4. Make america the dominant energy producer in the world, by far!
5. STOP OUTSOURCING, AND TURN THE UNITED STATES INTO A MANUFACTURING SUPERPOWER
6. large tax cuts for workers, and no tax on tips!
7. Defend our constitution, our bill of rights, and our fundamental freedoms, including freedom of speech, freedom of religion, and the right to keep and bear arms
8. Prevent world war three, restore peace in europe and in the middle east, and build a great iron dome missile defense shield over our entire country -- all made in america
9. End the weaponization of government against the american people

10. Stop the migrant crime epidemic, demolish the foreign drug cartels, crush gang violence, and lock up violent offenders
11. Rebuild our cities, including washington dc, making them safe, clean, and beautiful again.
12. Strengthen and modernize our military, making it, without question, the strongest and most powerful in the world
13. Keep the U.S. dollar as the world's reserve currency
14. Fight for and protect social security and medicare with no cuts, including no changes to the retirement age
15. Cancel the electric vehicle mandate and cut costly and burdensome regulations
16. Cut federal funding for any school pushing critical race theory, radical gender ideology, and other inappropriate racial, sexual, or political content on our children
17. Keep men out of women's sports
18. Deport pro-hamas radicals and make our college campuses safe and patriotic again
19. Secure our elections, including same day voting, voter identification, paper ballots, and proof of citizenship
20. Unite our country by bringing it to new and record levels of success

2024 GOP PLATFORM MAKE AMERICA GREAT AGAIN!

From Donald J. Trump Website
https://www.donaldjtrump.com/platform

Dedication:
To the Forgotten Men and Women of America

PREAMBLE America First: A Return to Common Sense

Our Nation's History is filled with the stories of brave men and women who gave everything they had to build America into the Greatest Nation in the History of the World. Generations of American Patriots have summoned the American Spirit of Strength, Determination, and Love of Country to overcome seemingly insurmountable challenges. The American People have proven time and again that we can overcome any obstacle and any force pitted against us.

In the early days of our Republic, the Founding Generation defeated what was then the most powerful Empire the World had ever seen. In the 20th Century, America vanquished Nazism and Fascism, and then triumphed over Soviet Communism after forty-four years of the Cold War.

But now we are a Nation in SERIOUS DECLINE. Our future, our identity, and our very way of life are under threat like never before. Today we must once again call upon the same American Spirit that led us to prevail through every challenge of the past if we are going to lead our Nation to a brighter future.

For decades, our politicians sold our jobs and livelihoods to the highest bidders overseas with unfair Trade Deals and a blind faith in the siren song of globalism. They insulated themselves from criticism and the consequences of their own bad actions, allowing our Borders to be overrun, our cities to be overtaken by crime, our System of Justice to be weaponized, and our young people to develop a sense of hopelessness and despair. They rejected our History and our Values. Quite simply, they did everything in their power to destroy our Country.

In 2016, President Donald J. Trump was elected as an unapologetic Champion of the American People. He reignited the American Spirit and called on us to renew our National Pride. His Policies spurred Historic Economic Growth, Job Creation, and a Resurgence of American Manufacturing. President Trump and the

Republican Party led America out of the pessimism induced by decades of failed leadership, showing us that the American People want Greatness for our Country again.

Yet after nearly four years of the Biden administration, America is now rocked by Raging Inflation, Open Borders, Rampant Crime, Attacks on our Children, and Global Conflict, Chaos, and Instability.

Like the Heroes who built and defended this Nation before us, we will never give up. We will restore our Nation of, by, and for the People. We will Make America Great Again.

We will be a Nation based on Truth, Justice, and Common Sense.

Common Sense tells us clearly, in President Trump's words, that "If we don't have a Border, we don't have a Country." Restoring sensible Border Security and Immigration Policy requires many steps, all of which would have been and indeed were taken for granted by prior Generations as obviously necessary and good. We must secure our Southern Border by completing the Border Wall that President Trump started. Hundreds of miles have already been built and work magnificently. The remaining Wall construction can be completed quickly, effectively, and inexpensively. We must also vigilantly check those who enter our Country by other routes and ensure that no one can enter our Country who does not have the Legal Right to do so, and we must deport the millions of illegal Migrants who Joe Biden has deliberately encouraged to invade our Country. We will start by prioritizing the most dangerous criminals and working with local Police. We must not allow Biden's Migrant 4 Invasion to alter our Country. It must not stand. Under the Trump Administration and a Republican Congress, it will be defeated immediately.

Common Sense tells us clearly that if we don't have Domestic Manufacturing with low Inflation, not only will our Economy—and even our Military Equipment and Supplies—be at the mercy of Foreign Nations, but our Towns, Communities, and People cannot thrive. The Republican Party must return to its roots as the Party of

Industry, Manufacturing, Infrastructure, and Workers. President Trump's economic policy to end Inflation and return Manufacturing Jobs is not only what the American Economy and American Workers need right now, it is also what they want right now.

Common Sense tells us clearly that we must unleash American Energy if we want to destroy Inflation and rapidly bring down prices, build the Greatest Economy in History, revive our Defense Industrial Base, fuel Emerging Industries, and establish the United States as the Manufacturing Superpower of the World. We will DRILL, BABY, DRILL and we will become Energy Independent, and even Dominant again. The United States has more liquid gold under our feet than any other Nation, and it's not even close. The Republican Party will harness that potential to power our future.

Common Sense tells us clearly that if we don't have a Strong Military, we won't be able to defend our interests and we will be at the mercy of Hostile Nations. The Policy of the Republican Party must be to ensure that America's Military is the strongest and best-equipped in the World—and that our Government uses that great strength sparingly, and only in clear instances where our National Interests are threatened.

Common Sense tells us clearly that the Republican Party must stand for Equal Treatment for All. Likewise, the Republican Party must ensure the equal application of law to all regardless of political affiliation or personal beliefs. Recent Democrat-led political persecutions threaten to destroy 250 years of American Principle and Practice and must be stopped.

America needs determined Republican Leadership at every level of Government to address the core threats to our very survival: Our disastrously Open Border, our weakened Economy, crippling restrictions on American Energy Production, our depleted Military, attacks on the American System of Justice, and much more.

To make clear our commitment, we offer to the American people the 2024 GOP Platform to Make America Great Again! It is a forward-looking Agenda that begins with the following twenty promises that we will accomplish very quickly when we win the White House and Republican Majorities in the House and Senate.

1. SEAL THE BORDER, AND STOP THE MIGRANT INVASION
2. CARRY OUT THE LARGEST DEPORTATION OPERATION IN AMERICAN HISTORY
3. END INFLATION, AND MAKE AMERICA AFFORDABLE AGAIN
4. MAKE AMERICA THE DOMINANT ENERGY PRODUCER IN THE WORLD, BY FAR!
5. STOP OUTSOURCING, AND TURN THE UNITED STATES INTO A MANUFACTURING SUPERPOWER
6. LARGE TAX CUTS FOR WORKERS, AND NO TAX ON TIPS!
7. DEFEND OUR CONSTITUTION, OUR BILL OF RIGHTS, AND OUR FUNDAMENTAL FREEDOMS, INCLUDING FREEDOM OF SPEECH, FREEDOM OF RELIGION, AND THE RIGHT TO KEEP AND BEAR ARMS
8. PREVENT WORLD WAR THREE, RESTORE PEACE IN EUROPE AND IN THE MIDDLE EAST, AND BUILD A GREAT IRON DOME MISSILE DEFENSE SHIELD OVER OUR ENTIRE COUNTRY -- ALL MADE IN AMERICA
9. END THE WEAPONIZATION OF GOVERNMENT AGAINST THE AMERICAN PEOPLE
10. STOP THE MIGRANT CRIME EPIDEMIC, DEMOLISH THE FOREIGN DRUG CARTELS, CRUSH GANG VIOLENCE, AND LOCK UP VIOLENT OFFENDERS
11. REBUILD OUR CITIES, INCLUDING WASHINGTON DC, MAKING THEM SAFE, CLEAN, AND BEAUTIFUL AGAIN.
12. STRENGTHEN AND MODERNIZE OUR MILITARY, MAKING IT, WITHOUT QUESTION, THE STRONGEST AND MOST POWERFUL IN THE WORLD
13. KEEP THE U.S. DOLLAR AS THE WORLD'S RESERVE CURRENCY
14. FIGHT FOR AND PROTECT SOCIAL SECURITY AND MEDICARE WITH NO CUTS, INCLUDING NO CHANGES TO THE RETIREMENT AGE
15. CANCEL THE ELECTRIC VEHICLE MANDATE AND CUT COSTLY AND BURDENSOME REGULATIONS
16. CUT FEDERAL FUNDING FOR ANY SCHOOL PUSHING CRITICAL RACE THEORY, RADICAL GENDER IDEOLOGY, AND OTHER INAPPROPRIATE RACIAL, SEXUAL, OR POLITICAL CONTENT ON OUR CHILDREN
17. KEEP MEN OUT OF WOMEN'S SPORTS

18. DEPORT PRO-HAMAS RADICALS AND MAKE OUR COLLEGE CAMPUSES SAFE AND PATRIOTIC AGAIN
19. SECURE OUR ELECTIONS, INCLUDING SAME DAY VOTING, VOTER IDENTIFICATION, PAPER BALLOTS, AND PROOF OF CITIZENSHIP
20. UNITE OUR COUNTRY BY BRINGING IT TO NEW AND RECORD LEVELS OF SUCCESS

*****

When America is united, confident, and committed to our principles, it will never fail.
Today and together, with Love for our Country, Faith in our People, and Trust in God's Good Grace, we will Make America Great Again!

Table of Contents

1. DEFEAT INFLATION, AND QUICKLY BRING DOWN ALL PRICES.
2. SEAL THE BORDER, AND STOP THE MIGRANT INVASION.
3. BUILD THE GREATEST ECONOMY IN HISTORY.
4. BRING BACK THE AMERICAN DREAM AND MAKE IT AFFORDABLE AGAIN FOR FAMILIES, YOUNG PEOPLE, AND EVERYONE.
5. PROTECT AMERICAN WORKERS AND FARMERS FROM UNFAIR TRADE.
6. PROTECT SENIORS.
7. CULTIVATE GREAT K-12 SCHOOLS LEADING TO GREAT JOBS AND GREAT LIVES FOR YOUNG PEOPLE.
8. BRING COMMON SENSE TO OUR GOVERNMENT AND RENEW THE PILLARS OF AMERICAN CIVILIZATION
9. GOVERNMENT OF, BY, AND FOR THE PEOPLE.
10. RETURN TO PEACE THROUGH STRENGTH.

CHAPTER ONE: DEFEAT INFLATION AND QUICKLY BRING DOWN ALL PRICES

Our Commitment:

The Republican Party will reverse the worst Inflation crisis in four decades that has crushed the middle class, devastated family budgets, and pushed the dream of homeownership out of reach for millions. We will defeat Inflation, tackle the costof-living crisis, improve fiscal sanity, restore price stability, and quickly bring down prices.

Inflation is a crushing tax on American families. History shows that Inflation will not magically disappear while policies remain the same. We commit to unleashing American Energy, reining in wasteful spending, cutting excessive Regulations, securing our Borders, and restoring Peace through Strength. Together, we will restore Prosperity, ensure Economic Security, and build a brighter future for American Workers and their families. Our dedication to these Policies will make America stronger, more resilient, and more prosperous than ever before.

1. Unleash American Energy

Under President Trump, the U.S. became the Number One Producer of Oil and Natural Gas in the World — and we will soon be again by lifting restrictions on American Energy Production and terminating the Socialist Green New Deal. Republicans will unleash Energy Production from all sources, including nuclear, to immediately slash Inflation and power American homes, cars, and factories with reliable, abundant, and affordable Energy.

2. Rein in Wasteful Federal Spending

Republicans will immediately stabilize the Economy by slashing wasteful Government spending and promoting Economic Growth.

3. Cut Costly and Burdensome Regulations

Republicans will reinstate President Trump's Deregulation Policies, which saved Americans $11,000 per household, and end Democrats' regulatory onslaught that disproportionately harms low- and middle-income households.

4. Stop Illegal Immigration

Republicans will secure the Border, deport Illegal Aliens, and reverse the Democrats' Open Borders Policies that have driven up the cost of Housing, Education, and Healthcare for American families.

5. Restore Peace through Strength

War breeds Inflation while geopolitical stability brings price stability. Republicans will end the global chaos and restore Peace through Strength, reducing geopolitical risks and lowering commodity prices.

CHAPTER TWO: SEAL THE BORDER, AND STOP THE MIGRANT INVASION

Our Commitment:

Republicans offer an aggressive plan to stop the open-border policies that have opened the floodgates to a tidal wave of illegal Aliens, deadly drugs, and Migrant Crime. We will end the Invasion at the Southern Border, restore Law and Order, protect American Sovereignty, and deliver a Safe and Prosperous Future for all Americans.

1. Secure the Border

Republicans will restore every Border Policy of the Trump administration and halt all releases of Illegal Aliens into the interior. We will complete the Border Wall, shift massive portions of Federal Law Enforcement to Immigration Enforcement, and use advanced technology to monitor and secure the Border. We will use all resources needed to stop the Invasion—including moving thousands of Troops currently stationed overseas to our own Southern Border. We will deploy the U.S.Navy to impose a full Fentanyl Blockade on the waters of our Region—boarding and inspecting ships to look for fentanyl and fentanyl precursors. Before we defend the Borders of Foreign Countries, we must first secure the Border of our Country.

2. Enforce Immigration Laws

Republicans will strengthen ICE, increase penalties for illegal entry and overstaying Visas, and reinstate "Remain in Mexico" and other Policies that helped reduce Illegal Immigration by historic lows in President Trump's first term. We will also invoke the Alien Enemies Act to remove all known or suspected gang members, drug dealers, or cartel members from the United States, ending the scourge of Illegal Alien gang violence once and for all. We will bring back the Travel Ban, and use Title 42 to end the child trafficking crisis by returning all trafficked children to their families in their Home Countries immediately.

3. Begin Largest Deportation Program in American History

President Trump and Republicans will reverse the Democrats' destructive Open Borders Policies that have allowed criminal gangs and Illegal Aliens from around the World to roam the United States without consequences. The Republican Party is committed to sending Illegal Aliens back home and removing those who have violated our Laws.

4. Strict Vetting

Republicans will use existing Federal Law to keep foreign Christian-hating Communists, Marxists, and Socialists out of America. Those who join our Country must love our Country. We will use extreme vetting to ensure that jihadists and jihadist sympathizers are not admitted.

5. Stop Sanctuary Cities

Republicans will cut federal Funding to sanctuary jurisdictions that release dangerous Illegal Alien criminals onto our streets, rather than handing them over to ICE. We will require local cooperation with Federal Immigration Enforcement.

6. Ensure Our Legal Immigration System Puts American Workers First

Republicans will prioritize Merit-based immigration, ensuring those admitted to our Country contribute positively to our Society and Economy, and never become a drain on Public Resources. We will end Chain Migration, and put American Workers first!

CHAPTER THREE: BUILD THE GREATEST ECONOMY IN HISTORY

Our Commitment:

American Workers are the most productive, talented, and innovative on Earth. The only thing holding them back is the suffocating policies of the Democrat Party. Our America First Economic Agenda rests on five pillars: Slashing Regulations, cutting Taxes, securing Fair Trade Deals, ensuring Reliable and Abundant Low Cost Energy, and championing Innovation. Together, we will restore Economic Prosperity and Opportunity for all Americans.

1. Cut Regulations

Republicans will slash Regulations that stifle Jobs, Freedom, Innovation and make everything more expensive. We will implement Transparency and Common Sense in rulemaking.

2. Make Trump Tax Cuts Permanent and No Tax on Tips

Republicans will make permanent the provisions of the Trump Tax Cuts and Jobs Act that doubled the standard deduction, expanded the Child Tax Credit, and spurred Economic Growth for all Americans. We will eliminate Taxes on Tips for millions of Restaurant and Hospitality Workers, and pursue additional Tax Cuts.

3. Fair and Reciprocal Trade Deals

Republicans will continue forging an America First Trade Policy as set forth in Chapter 5, standing up to Countries that cheat and prioritizing American Producers over Foreign Outsourcers. We will bring our critical Supply Chains back home. President Trump turned American Trade Policy around, protecting U.S. Producers, and renegotiating failed agreements.

4. Reliable and Abundant Low Cost Energy

Republicans will increase Energy Production across the board, streamline permitting, and end market-distorting restrictions on Oil, Natural Gas, and Coal. The Republican Party will once again make America Energy Independent, and then Energy Dominant, lowering Energy prices even below the record lows achieved during President Trump's first term.

5. Champion Innovation

Republicans will pave the way for future Economic Greatness by leading the World in Emerging Industries.

Crypto

Republicans will end Democrats' unlawful and unAmerican Crypto crackdown and oppose the creation of a Central Bank Digital Currency. We will defend the right to mine Bitcoin, and ensure every American has the right to self-custody of their Digital Assets, and transact free from Government Surveillance and Control.

Artificial Intelligence (AI)

We will repeal Joe Biden's dangerous Executive Order that hinders AI Innovation, and imposes Radical Leftwing ideas on the development of this technology. In its place, Republicans support AI Development rooted in Free Speech and Human Flourishing.
Expanding Freedom, Prosperity and Safety in Space

Under Republican Leadership, the United States will create a robust Manufacturing Industry in Near Earth Orbit, send American Astronauts back to the Moon, and onward to Mars, and enhance partnerships with the rapidly expanding Commercial Space sector to revolutionize our ability to access, live in, and develop assets in Space.

CHAPTER FOUR: BRING BACK THE AMERICAN DREAM AND MAKE IT AFFORDABLE AGAIN FOR FAMILIES, YOUNG PEOPLE, AND EVERYONE

Our Commitment:

Republicans offer a plan to make the American Dream affordable again. We commit to reducing Housing, Education, and Healthcare costs, while lowering everyday expenses, and increasing opportunities.

1. Housing Affordability

To help new home buyers, Republicans will reduce mortgage rates by slashing Inflation, open limited portions of Federal Lands to allow for new home construction, promote homeownership through Tax Incentives and support for first-time buyers, and cut unnecessary Regulations that raise housing costs.

2. Accessible Higher Education

To reduce the cost of Higher Education, Republicans will support the creation of additional, drastically more affordable alternatives to a traditional four-year College degree.

3. Affordable Healthcare

Healthcare and prescription drug costs are out of control. Republicans will increase Transparency, promote Choice and Competition, and expand access to new Affordable Healthcare and prescription drug options. We will protect Medicare, and ensure Seniors receive the care they need without being burdened by excessive costs.

4. Lower Everyday Costs

Republicans will reduce the Regulatory burden, lower Energy costs, and promote Economic Policies that drive down the cost of living and prices for everyday goods and services.

CHAPTER FIVE: PROTECT AMERICAN WORKERS AND FARMERS FROM UNFAIR TRADE

Our Commitment:

The Republican Party stands for a patriotic "America First" Economic Policy. Republicans offer a robust plan to protect American Workers, Farmers, and Industries from unfair Foreign Competition. We commit to rebalancing Trade, securing Strategic Independence, and revitalizing Manufacturing. We will prioritize Domestic Production, and ensure National Independence in essential goods and services. Together, we will build a Strong, Self-reliant, and Prosperous America.

1. Rebalance Trade

Our Trade deficit in goods has grown to over $1 Trillion Dollars a year. Republicans will support baseline Tariffs on Foreignmade goods, pass the Trump Reciprocal Trade Act, and respond to unfair Trading practices. As Tariffs on Foreign Producers go up, Taxes on American Workers, Families, and Businesses can come down.

2. Secure Strategic Independence from China

Republicans will revoke China's Most Favored Nation status, phase out imports of essential goods, and stop China from buying American Real Estate and Industries.

3. Save the American Auto Industry

Republicans will revive the U.S. Auto Industry by reversing harmful Regulations, canceling Biden's Electric Vehicle and other Mandates, and preventing the importation of Chinese vehicles.

4. Bring Home Critical Supply Chains

Republicans will bring critical Supply Chains back to the U.S., ensuring National Security and Economic Stability, while also creating Jobs and raising Wages for American Workers.

5. Buy American and Hire American

Republicans will strengthen Buy American and Hire American Policies, banning companies that outsource jobs from doing business with the Federal Government.

6. Become the Manufacturing Superpower

By protecting American Workers from unfair Foreign Competition and unleashing American Energy, Republicans will restore American Manufacturing, creating Jobs, Wealth, and Investment.

CHAPTER SIX: PROTECT SENIORS

Our Commitment:

President Trump has made absolutely clear that he will not cut one penny from Medicare or Social Security. American Citizens work hard their whole lives, contributing to Social Security and Medicare. These programs are promises to our Seniors, ensuring they can live their golden years with dignity. Republicans will protect these vital programs and ensure Economic Stability. We will work with our Great Seniors, in order to allow them to be active and healthy. We commit to safeguarding the future for our Seniors and all American families.

1. Protect Social Security

Social Security is a lifeline for millions of Retirees, yet corrupt politicians have robbed Social Security to fund their pet projects. Republicans will restore Economic Stability to ensure the long-term sustainability of Social Security.

2. Strengthen Medicare

Republicans will protect Medicare's finances from being financially crushed by the Democrat plan to add tens of millions of new illegal immigrants to the rolls of Medicare. We vow to strengthen Medicare for future generations.

3. Support Active and Healthy Living

Republicans will support increased focus on Chronic Disease prevention and management, Long-Term Care, and Benefit flexibility. We will expand access to Primary Care and support

Policies that help Seniors remain in their homes and maintain Financial Security.

4. Protect Care at Home for the Elderly

Republicans will shift resources back to at-home Senior Care, overturn disincentives that lead to Care Worker shortages, and support unpaid Family Caregivers through Tax Credits and reduced red tape.

5. Protect Economic Foundations for Supporting Seniors

Republicans will tackle Inflation, unleash American Energy, restore Economic Growth, and secure our Borders to preserve Social Security and Medicare funding for the next Generation and beyond. We will ensure these programs remain solvent long into the future by reversing harmful Democrat policies and unleashing a new Economic Boom.

CHAPTER SEVEN: CULTIVATE GREAT K-12 SCHOOLS LEADING TO GREAT JOBS AND GREAT LIVES FOR YOUNG PEOPLE

Our Commitment:

Republicans offer a plan to cultivate great K-12 schools, ensure safe learning environments free from political meddling, and restore Parental Rights. We commit to an Education System that empowers students, supports families, and promotes American Values. Our Education System must prepare students for successful lives and well-paying jobs.

1. Great Principals and Great Teachers

Republicans will support schools that focus on Excellence and Parental Rights. We will support ending Teacher Tenure, adopting Merit pay, and allowing various publicly supported Educational models.

2. Universal School Choice

Republicans believe families should be empowered to choose the best Education for their children. We support Universal School Choice in every State in America. We will expand 529 Education Savings Accounts and support Homeschooling Families equally.

3. Prepare Students for Jobs and Careers

Republicans will emphasize Education to prepare students for great jobs and careers, supporting project-based learning and schools that offer meaningful work experience. We will expose politicized education models and fund proven career training programs.

4. Safe, Secure, and Drug-Free Schools

Republicans will support overhauling standards on school discipline, advocate for immediate suspension of violent students, and support hardening schools to help keep violence away from our places of learning.

5. Restore Parental Rights

Republicans will restore Parental Rights in Education, and enforce our Civil Rights Laws to stop schools from discriminating on the basis of Race. We trust Parents!

6. Knowledge and Skills, Not CRT and Gender Indoctrination

Republicans will ensure children are taught fundamentals like Reading, History, Science, and Math, not Leftwing propaganda. We will defund schools that engage in inappropriate political indoctrination of our children using Federal Taxpayer Dollars.

7. Promote Love of Country with Authentic Civics Education

Republicans will reinstate the 1776 Commission, promote Fair and Patriotic Civics Education, and veto efforts to nationalize Civics Education. We will support schools that teach America's Founding Principles and Western Civilization.

8. Freedom to Pray

Republicans will champion the First Amendment Right to Pray and Read the Bible in school, and stand up to those who violate the Religious Freedoms of American students.

9. Return Education to the States

The United States spends more money per pupil on Education than any other Country in the World, and yet we are at the bottom of every educational list in terms of results. We are going to close the Department of Education in Washington, D.C. and send it back to the States, where it belongs, and let the States run our educational system as it should be run. Our Great Teachers, who are so important to the future wellbeing of our Country, will be cherished and protected by the Republican Party so that they can do the job of educating our students that they so dearly want to do. It is our goal to bring Education in the United States to the highest level, one that it has never attained before!

CHAPTER EIGHT: BRING COMMON SENSE TO GOVERNMENT AND RENEW THE PILLARS OF AMERICAN CIVILIZATION

Our Commitment:

Republicans offer a plan to renew American Civilization with Common Sense Policies that supports families, restores Law and Order, cares for Veterans, promotes beauty, and honors American History. We commit to strengthening the Foundations of our Society for a brighter future.

1. Empower American Families

Republicans will promote a Culture that values the Sanctity of Marriage, the blessings of childhood, the foundational role of families, and supports working parents. We will end policies that punish families.

2. Rebuild Our Cities and Restore Law and Order

Republicans will restore safety in our neighborhoods by replenishing Police Departments, restoring Common Sense Policing, and protecting Officers from frivolous lawsuits. We will stand up to Marxist Prosecutors, vigorously defend the Right of every American to live in peace, and we will compassionately address homelessness to restore order to our streets.

3. Make Washington D.C. the Safest and Most Beautiful Capital City

Republicans will reassert greater Federal Control over Washington, DC to restore Law and Order in our Capital City, and ensure Federal Buildings and Monuments are well-maintained.

4. Take Care of Our Veterans

Republicans will end luxury housing and Taxpayer benefits for Illegal Immigrants and use those savings to shelter and treat homeless Veterans. We will restore Trump Administration reforms to expand Veterans' Healthcare Choices, protect Whistleblowers, and hold accountable poorly performing employees not giving our Veterans the care they deserve.

5. Make Colleges and Universities Sane and Affordable

Republicans will fire Radical Left accreditors, drive down Tuition costs, restore Due Process protections, and pursue Civil Rights cases against Schools that discriminate.

6. Combat Antisemitism

Republicans condemn antisemitism, and support revoking Visas of Foreign Nationals who support terrorism and jihadism. We will hold accountable those who perpetrate violence against Jewish people.

7. Overcome the Crisis in Liberal Arts Education

Republicans support the restoration of Classic Liberal Arts Education.

8. Restore American Beauty

Republicans will promote beauty in Public Architecture and preserve our Natural Treasures. We will build cherished symbols of our Nation, and restore genuine Conservation efforts.

9. Honor American History

Republicans celebrate our Great American Heroes and are proud that the Story of America makes everyone free. We will organize a National Celebration to mark the 250th Anniversary of the Founding of the United States of America.

CHAPTER NINE: GOVERNMENT OF, BY, AND FOR THE PEOPLE

Our Commitment:

Republicans will offer a clear, precise, and USA oriented plan to stop the Radical Left Democrats' Weaponization of Government and its Assault on American Liberty. We will restore Government of, by, and for the People, ensuring Accountability, protecting Individual Liberties, and fixing our once very corrupt Elections. We commit to upholding the Constitution of the United States, appointing judges who respect the rule of law, and defending the Rights of all Americans to Life, Liberty, and the Pursuit of Happiness. We will maintain the Supreme Court as it was always meant to be, at 9 Justices. We will not allow the Democrat Party to increase this number, as they would like to do, by 4, 6, 8, 10, and even 12 Justices. We will block them at every turn.

1. Republicans Will Stop Woke and Weaponized Government

We will hold accountable those who have misused the power of Government to unjustly prosecute their Political Opponents. We will declassify Government records, root out wrongdoers, and fire corrupt employees.

2. Republicans Will Dismantle Censorship & Protect Free Speech

We will ban the Federal Government from colluding with anyone to censor Lawful Speech, defund institutions engaged in censorship, and hold accountable all bureaucrats involved with illegal censoring. We will protect Free Speech online.

3. Republicans Will Defend Religious Liberty

We are the defenders of the First Amendment Right to Religious Liberty. It protects the Right not only to Worship according to the dictates of Conscience, but also to act in accordance with those Beliefs, not just in places of Worship, but in everyday life. Our ranks include men and women from every Faith and Tradition, and we respect the Right of every American to follow his or her deeply held Beliefs. To protect Religious Liberty, Republicans support a new Federal Task Force on Fighting Anti-Christian Bias that will investigate all forms of illegal discrimination, harassment, and persecution against Christians in America.

4. Republicans Will Protect and Defend a Vote of the People, from within the States, on the Issue of Life

We proudly stand for families and Life. We believe that the 14th Amendment to the Constitution of the United States guarantees that no person can be denied Life or Liberty without Due Process, and that the States are, therefore, free to pass Laws protecting those Rights. After 51 years, because of us, that power has been given to the States and to a vote of the People. We will oppose Late Term Abortion, while supporting mothers and policies that advance Prenatal Care, access to Birth Control, and IVF (fertility treatments).

5. Republicans Will End Left-wing Gender Insanity

We will keep men out of women's sports, ban Taxpayer funding for sex change surgeries, and stop Taxpayer-funded Schools from promoting gender transition, reverse Biden's radical rewrite of Title IX Education Regulations, and restore protections for women and girls.

6. Republicans Will Ensure Election Integrity

We will implement measures to secure our Elections, including Voter ID, highly sophisticated paper ballots, proof of Citizenship, and same day Voting. We will not allow the Democrats to give Voting Rights to illegal Aliens.

7. Republicans Will Protect Americans in the Territories.

The territories of Guam, the Commonwealth of the Northern Mariana Islands, American Samoa, the U.S. Virgin Islands, and Puerto Rico are of vital importance to our National Security, and we welcome their greater participation in all aspects of the political process.

CHAPTER TEN: RETURN TO PEACE THROUGH STRENGTH

Our Commitment:

Keeping the American People safe requires a strong America. The Biden administration's weak Foreign Policy has made us less safe and a laughingstock all over the World. The Republican Plan is to return Peace through Strength, rebuilding our Military and Alliances, countering China, defeating terrorism, building an Iron Dome Missile Defense Shield, promoting American Values, securing our Homeland and Borders, and reviving our Defense Industrial Base. We will build a Military bigger, better, and stronger than ever before. Our full commitment is to protecting America and ensuring a safe and prosperous future for all.

1. The National Interest

Republicans will promote a Foreign Policy centered on the most essential American Interests, starting with protecting the American Homeland, our People, our Borders, our Great American Flag, and our Rights under God.

2. Modernize the Military

Republicans will ensure our Military is the most modern, lethal and powerful Force in the World. We will invest in cuttingedge research and advanced technologies, including an Iron Dome Missile Defense Shield, support our Troops with higher pay, and get woke Leftwing Democrats fired as soon as possible.

3. Strengthen Alliances

Republicans will strengthen Alliances by ensuring that our Allies must meet their obligations to invest in our Common Defense and by restoring Peace to Europe. We will stand with Israel, and seek peace in the Middle East. We will rebuild our Alliance Network in the Region to ensure a future of Peace, Stability, and Prosperity. Likewise, we will champion Strong, Sovereign, and Independent Nations in the Indo-Pacific, thriving in Peace and Commerce with others.

4. Strengthen Economic, Military, and Diplomatic Capabilities

Republicans will strengthen Economic, Military, and Diplomatic capabilities to protect the American way of life from the malign influences of Countries that stand against us around the World.

5. Defend America's Borders

Against all odds, President Trump has completed Hundreds of Miles of Wall, and he will quickly finish the job. Republicans will mobilize Military personnel and assets as necessary to crack down hard on the cartels that traffic drugs and people into our Country.

6. Revive our Industrial Base

Our Industrial Base is critical to ensuring good jobs for our people but also the reliable production of vital Defense platforms and supplies. Our Policy must be to revive our Industrial Base, with priority on Defense-critical industries. Equipment and parts critical to American Security must be MADE IN THE USA.

7. Protect Critical Infrastructure

Republicans will use all tools of National Power to protect our Nation's Critical Infrastructure and Industrial Base from malicious cyber actors. This will be a National Priority, and we will both raise the Security Standards for our Critical Systems and Networks and defend them against bad actors.

BOOK DESCRIPTION:

In **"Trump Should Triumph,"** author Michael Cage presents a compelling and passionate argument for why Donald J. Trump's leadership is vital for the future of America. Drawing from Trump's proven track record during his presidency (2017-2021), this book delves into the former president's achievements, highlighting his bold economic strategies, dedication to national security, and unrelenting patriotism.

Chapter by chapter, Cage exposes the erosion of American values under the current administration, focusing on border security, traditional values, and the growing cultural confusion surrounding gender identity. With a powerful critique of the Harris/Biden administration's failed promises, Cage contrasts Trump's steady hand and vision with the chaos and instability America now faces.

In **"A Heart of Patriotism,"** Cage explores Trump's personal sacrifices, illustrating the depth of his commitment to the country, while **"The Economy, Then and Now"** reveals the stark differences between the prosperity under Trump's leadership and the economic decline that has followed. Cage's insightful look into the top policies of both parties gives readers a clear understanding of the political battleground on which America's future rests.

With clarity and urgency, **"Trump Should Triumph"** delivers a call to action, rallying readers to recognize the strength of Trump's legacy and the hope it holds for restoring American greatness. For anyone concerned about the nation's future, this book is a must-read.